holiday *Decorations*

holiday *Decorations*

A COLLECTION OF
INSPIRED GIFTS, RECIPES,
AND DECORATING IDEAS

By Genevieve A. Sterbenz
Photography by
Steven Mays

SMITHMARK

This edition published in 1998 by SMITHMARK Publishers,
a division of U.S. Media Holdings, Inc.,
115 West 18th Street, New York, NY 10011.

SMITHMARK books are available for bulk purchase for sales promotion and premium use.
For details, write or call the manager of special sales, SMITHMARK Publishers,
115 West 18th Street, New York, NY 10011.

Text and Project Design: Genevieve A. Sterbenz
Photography: Steven Mays
Editor: Kristen Schilo, Gato & Maui Productions
Design: Galen Smith
Stylist: Sylvia Lachter
Technical Writer: Mary Ann Hall
Photo, p. 44, by Sandra Mojas

ISBN: 0-7651-0838-0

Printed in Hong Kong

10 9 8 7 6 5 4 3 2 1

Library of Congress Cataloging-in-Publication Data

Sterbenz, Genevieve A.
    Holiday decorations : a collection of inspired gifts, recipes, and
decorating ideas / by Genevieve A. Sterbenz ; photography by Steven
Mays.
        p.   cm.
    ISBN 0-7651-0838-0 (alk. paper)
    1. Christmas decorations.   2. Handicraft.   I. Title.
TT900.C4S732   1998
745.594' 12--dc21
                                                        98-23423
                                                        CIP

Dedication

For Dean, the movie star, Catherine, the queen o' sass, and Grace, the most fabulous woman I know south of the Mason-Dixon line.

Acknowledgments

I would like to thank Steven Mays and Sylvia Lachter for all of their hard work and for their willingness to burn the midnight oil with me, and to Kristen Schilo for her dedication, support, and laughter. Thanks to Mary Ann Hall and Galen Smith for doing beautiful work on the strictest of deadlines. I would like to thank my mother for her love and guidance, my father for "John's Shipping and Storage," my brother for the extended use of his computer, and my sister for her musical cooking expertise. Thanks to Catherine Neuner for testing all the recipes and to Sarah Jane Bacall for her bead work. A special thanks to Meredith Walsh for helping us make our Christmas table complete and to Wolfman-Gold & Good Company in Soho, NY.

doors & windows

2

Introduction

1

the mantel

3

My First Ornament

When I was three years old, my mother sat with me at the kitchen table in front of some shredded newspaper, a bowl of watered down Elmer's Glue, and some red paint. Following my mother's lead, I began dipping the strips of newspaper in the glue and wrapping them around a piece of newspaper that I had balled up. When I was happy with the size of the ball I had molded, my mother set it aside to dry. Once the ball had dried, I covered it with two coats of red paint, pushed a piece of wire in it for hanging, and hung it on our tree. It was the first ornament I had ever made.

Now, at Christmas time, when I take my red papier-mâché ball out of the holiday ornament box and unwrap it from the tissue that protects it, I study it for a while. I attempt to read the story that was printed on the newspaper, trying to gain some insight into what was going on in the world during that December of 1974.

Every Christmas since I made that red ball, my family has gotten together to make new ornaments for our tree. There was the year of the felt mice in walnut shells, the yellow pompom "superbird" with a red cape that my brother made, and the construction paper Christmas tree that my younger sister decorated with Styrofoam peanuts and raisins. Although my brother, sister, and I are adults now and we are living on our own, we still look forward to getting together to make ornaments for our parents' tree. This past Christmas we made the Glitterball Ornaments that are included in "The Tree" chapter.

We continue this family tradition every year, despite the fact that we all lead busy lives. We use fun materials and get instant results, and that is what I wanted this book to be all about. *Holiday Decorations* is filled with projects that are simple to do and that use materials that are familiar and easy to find. Many of the projects can be completed in under an hour, regardless of one's skill level. In addition, each of these decorating ideas can be tailored to your own home by choosing different colors or by adapting the size of the project.

Holiday Decorations was a labor of love, one that began with the traditions of my childhood. It is my hope that you will be inspired by this collection, so that you may begin new traditions of your own.

doors & windows

2

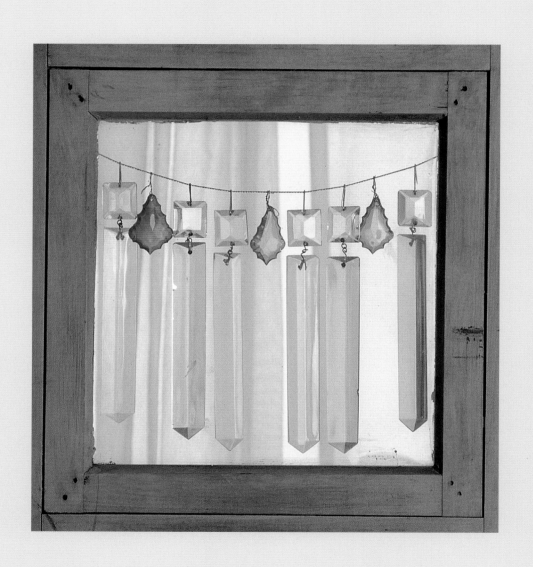

*T*he windows and doorways to your home are the prelude to the warmth and beauty of the atmosphere within. They create a lasting first impression and the sweet expectation of what will follow when passing through them. Properly dressed, windows can transform a home into a glowing beacon on a cold night, and a door into a passage to sustenance and rest.

In this chapter, you will find simple, yet sophisticated ways to welcome your guests from the moment they arrive at your doorstep. Each unique accent requires only your imagination, a little bit of time and money, and yet transforms your entryways beautifully.

The holidays are the perfect reason and ideal opportunity to have some fun and be creative. Whether it's the fragrant, natural beauty of the Lemon and Eucalyptus Leaf Wreath or the brilliant splash of scarlet from the Red Berry Wreath, you will discover the perfect decoration to suit your taste and to complement your holiday décor.

Elegant patterns can be created by simply stringing chandelier crystals and beads along window panes. These window ornaments will be appreciated when viewed from the outside, as they sparkle and reflect interior light, or from the inside, as they cast rainbows and beautiful shadows from the sun. The glittering fruits on the Glitter Fruit Tie Back create a festive window accent that can be tailored easily to fit your needs.

Use the ideas found in this chapter to determine which styles and materials work best in your home; then echo these accents as you begin to create your interior designs. By starting with your doors and windows, you can build a framework and set a tone for the rest of your holiday decorating.

Fruit Wreath

PLASTIC FRUIT IS INEXPENSIVE AND AVAILABLE
IN MOST CRAFT STORES. USING ONLY HOT GLUE,
YOU CAN LAYER SEVERAL VARIETIES OF FRUIT,
MIXING COLORS, SIZES, AND TEXTURES TO
QUICKLY CREATE A WREATH WITH GREAT
VISUAL IMPACT.

TIME REQUIRED: 1 HOUR

MATERIALS NEEDED
14-inch length medium-gauge florist wire
Straw wreath form
35 silk leaves, 3-4 inches long
(may not be needed if fruits have their own foliage)
Hot glue gun and glue sticks
Plastic fruit:

4 pears, green and yellow	3 stems blueberries or blackberries
5 strawberries	4 plums
5 apples	4 oranges
7 grape clusters	3 pomegranates
5 cherry clusters	5 gold pine cones

Floral pins (optional)

DIRECTIONS

STEP 1   To create hanging loop, wrap wire around
wreath form at 12 o'clock position; bring ends to back and
twist ends against wreath to secure. Twist one end of wire
into loop and secure against wreath back.

STEP 2   Attach single leaves around outside perimeter of
wreath with hot glue, allowing ends to radiate and overlap;
repeat around inner edge.

STEP 3   Use hot glue to attach large pieces of fruit at 11
o'clock, 2 o'clock, 4 o'clock, and 8 o'clock, positioning fruit
upright, or on its side for variety. Continue adding clusters
of smaller varieties around large pieces.

STEP 4   Stand back from wreath to assess distribution of
fruit color and size, adding contrasting pieces as needed.

STEP 5   To finish, intersperse additional leaves between
fruit, using hot glue to secure. Secure further with floral
pins, if needed.

Red Berry Wreath

THE RICH RED COLOR AND SIMPLE GEOMETRY OF THIS
TRADITIONAL WREATH CAN BE USED TO DECORATE THE HOME
FOR YEARS TO COME.

TIME REQUIRED: 1 $\frac{1}{2}$ HOURS

MATERIALS NEEDED

Newspaper

10-inch-diameter vine wreath base

Sponge brush

Red acrylic paint

Florist wire

4 packages red canella berries

Pruning shears

Hot glue gun and glue sticks

DIRECTIONS

STEP 1   Protect work surface with newspaper.

STEP 2   Use sponge brush to paint vine wreath red; let dry.

STEP 3   Use florist wire to make hanging loop at back of wreath by pulling wire through some of vines and twisting to secure.

STEP 4   Use shears to cut sprigs of berries from main stem; set aside sprigs and loose berries.

STEP 5   To decorate wreath, position one berry sprig on front of wreath, using hot glue to secure end. Continue gluing additional branches, overlapping vine wreath and other glued sprigs until wreath is concealed and berries are multi-layered. (Use loose berries to cover cut end of stems or holes between sprigs.)

STEP 6   Let dry. Completed wreath will be approximately 14 inches in diameter.

Glitter Fruit Tieback

THIS SPARKLING TIEBACK CAN BE CUSTOMIZED TO MATCH ANY COLOR SCHEME AND TO FIT ANY WINDOW DRESSING; JUST SELECT GLITTER IN COORDINATING COLORS, AND FRUIT PIECES WHICH ARE IN PROPORTION TO THE DESIRED SIZE.

TIME REQUIRED: 2 HOURS

MATERIALS NEEDED

Newspaper

4-5-inch plastic-coated Styrofoam fruit with wire stems

(pictured here are 4 pomegranates and 2 pears)

Aleene's Tacky Thin-bodied Glue

Sponge brush

Glitter: red, gold, dark green, lime green

(approximately one 11-gram vial per piece of fruit)

8 large round leaves with wire stems

4 narrow leaves with wire stems

Green florist wire

Red and gold wire-edged ribbon

DIRECTIONS

STEP 1   Protect work surface with newspaper.

STEP 2   Select first piece of fruit. Squeeze glue directly on to surface of fruit. Use sponge brush to spread glue into thin, even layer.

STEP 3   Sprinkle desired color of glitter over fruit, rotating stem until completely covered. Add more glue and glitter as needed to coat. Reuse extra glitter by picking up edges of newspaper to collect glitter in center. Pour extra glitter into bowl or paper cup.

STEP 4   On same piece of fruit, apply glue to stem and leaves. Sprinkle dark green glitter on larger leaves and lime green on smaller ones. Bend stem into hook and hang to dry.

STEP 5   Repeat Steps 2 through 4 for remaining fruit and leaves. Allow all pieces to dry 1 hour.

STEP 6   To assemble tieback, select one pear and one pomegranate and hold them with stems crossed in opposite directions. Twist stems around each other 3 times, leaving one stem jutting out to right and one to left. Continue adding pieces of fruit by twisting them onto the stem pointing to the left, with each new stem also pointing toward the left.

STEP 7   When all fruit is added, one stem should be extending out to right, and 2 or 3 extending out to left. Secure stray stems to central stem with florist wire. If necessary, add glitter to any portions that may have rubbed off during twisting.

STEP 8   When tieback is completely dry, shape it by bending pieces of fruit into desired position. Use fruit and leaves to hide central wire stem. Tie a ribbon bow at left-hand side next to last piece of fruit. Use fingers to shape and fluff bow.

STEP 9   Bend ends of central stem around curtain. Twist ends together at back and squeeze gently to secure in place.

Antique Chandelier Crystal Window

MAKE LOVELY WINDOW PATTERNS BY STRINGING SINGLE CHANDELIER CRYSTALS AND COLORED
GLASS BEADS ALONG A THIN CORD. USE SIMPLE, SYMMETRICAL ARRANGEMENTS TO CREATE
A DELICATE EFFECT.

TIME REQUIRED: 1 ½ HOURS

MATERIALS NEEDED

Eye hooks

Hammer

⅛-inch-thick gold cord

Chandelier crystals

Colored crystal beads (pictured here: red, green, lime green,
eggplant, lavender, yellow, and burnt sienna)

Scissors

Note: the number of crystals and cord required for
this project depends on how many panes of the window you
plan to decorate. The project pictured, *right*, required 22
chandelier crystals and 27 colored crystal beads.
The cording should also be 4 inches longer than width of the
window pane.

DIRECTIONS

STEP 1   Place an eye hook on right side of window frame,
positioning hook 1 inch away from pane and 1 inch from
top. Tap gently with hammer to start, then screw rest of the
hook in by hand.

STEP 2   Repeat Step 1 on left side matching height and
position of the first eye hook.

STEP 3   Tie one end of cord to eye hook on right side. Tie
double and triple knots to secure.

STEP 4   String crystals one by one, alternating between
chandelier crystals and colored crystal beads.

STEP 5   Pull cord across window to hang at the desired
height; tie securely to left side eye hook. Cut away any
excess cord.

STEP 6   Repeat Steps 1 through 5 for as many window
panes as you want to decorate.

Lemon and Eucalyptus Wreath

WELCOME YOUR HOLIDAY VISITORS WITH THIS SUMPTUOUS, DOOR WREATH. HEARTY LEMON LEAVES AND THE NARROW LEAVES OF SEEDED EUCALYPTUS ARE COMBINED WITH SIMPLE CONSTRUCTION TECHNIQUES TO CREATE THIS BEAUTIFUL, UNTAMED ARRANGEMENT.

TIME REQUIRED: 1 ½ HOURS

MATERIALS NEEDED

4 bunches fresh lemon leaves
(approximately 25-30 stems per bunch)
4 bunches fresh seeded eucalyptus
(approximately 25-30 stems per bunch)
Garden shears
Bucket
Floralife plant food
Newspaper
Ruler
Medium-gauge green florist wire
Wire cutters
18-inch-diameter straw wreath form
6 floral pins

DIRECTIONS

STEP 1   Condition fresh greens by stripping off bottom leaves from stems. Submerge stems in bucket of water that has been treated with Floralife. Let set overnight.

STEP 2   Protect work surface with newspaper and lay out all stems to assess condition and size of leafy branches.

STEP 3   Use ruler and shears to measure and cut the eucalyptus and lemon leaf stems 10-inches long.

STEP 4   To make one bouquet, gather 6-8 stems of one variety together in one hand, arranging leafy heads in fan-shaped cluster. Use wire to bind stems together, winding wire 6-8 times until stems are secure; cut wire and set bouquet aside. Repeat to make 10 bouquets of each variety.

STEP 5   To bind bouquets to wreath front, use a clock-face orientation. Lay one lemon leaf bouquet on wreath form at 12 o'clock, stems pointing to 11 o'clock; bind in place using wire. Do not cut wire.

STEP 6   Position second lemon leaf bouquet next to first, placing leafy end over stems of first bouquet. Use wire to secure. Follow with 2 bouquets of eucalyptus. (Stems may have to be trimmed shorter as you work around the curve of the wreath.)

STEP 7   Repeat Steps 5 and 6 to bind all bouquets, alternating varieties after each 2 bouquets.

STEP 8   If needed, cover thin areas with small bouquets and secure using floral pins. The final size of wreath is approximately 27 inches in diameter.

Fresh Greens and Fruit Garland

THIS GARLAND IS PERFECT FOR ANY AREA OF THE HOUSE; DRAPE IT OVER A DOOR, AROUND A MIRROR, ALONG A BANISTER, OR ACROSS A WINDOW. THE USE OF STURDY PLANT MATERIALS ALLOWS IT TO LAST ABOUT TWO WEEKS IN ITS LIVE STATE AND WHEN DRIED, ITS COLOR CHANGES TO SAGE AND HUNTER GREEN, MAKING IT A DECORATION TO BE ENJOYED THROUGHOUT THE YEAR.

TIME REQUIRED: 1 ½ HOURS

MATERIALS NEEDED

64 leafy stems
(pictured here: boxwood, lemon leaves, and ruscus)
Bucket
Pruning shears
Newspaper
Gold acrylic spray paint
12 pine cones
Florist wire
Wire cutters
6-foot-long cotton laundry rope
6 plastic apples
6 plastic pears
3 yards wire-edged gold ribbon

DIRECTIONS

STEP 1   Plunge greens in bucket of water until ready to use.

STEP 2   Prepare plant material by cutting 6-8-inch sections from leafy stems or branches.

STEP 3   Protect work surface with newspaper. Apply a spare, glistening layer of gold paint to leafy branches and pine cones by spraying in light circular motion; let paint dry.

STEP 4   Collect 4-6 stems of mixed foliage and bind into individual bouquets using florist wire. Bind remaining foliage into bouquets.

STEP 5   Bind bouquets to rope. Hold rope at one end with hand and lay first bouquet on rope with leaves extending 4 inches beyond end of rope. Secure stems of bouquet to rope by wrapping both with wire. Do not cut wire.

STEP 6   Conceal stems of attached bouquet with leafy head of second bouquet; Bind in place with wire. Continue adding all but 3-4 bouquets, overlapping stems of previous bouquet with head of next bouquet until rope is concealed.

STEP 7   For last bouquet on rope, lay leafy section in opposite direction to conceal end of rope; bind in place. If necessary, push in additional greenery or attach small bouquets to fill out any bare spots.

STEP 8   To decorate garland, use wire to attach fruit and pine cones. If desired, test fit in planned display area to determine position of decorations.

STEP 9   To complete, lay ribbon along garland, pushing sections of ribbon between branches to secure; allowing ends to cascade down naturally.

Caution: Do not display near open flame or heat.

the mantel

3

*A*dorning the mantel, especially during the holiday season, is a timeless tradition. A mantel provides a wonderful setting for which to display artwork, candles, photos, and collections. Decorating this area often involves the basic processes of arranging and rearranging these elements, as well as creating new ones. This chapter will give you new ideas for creating mantel displays that use common and inexpensive items and result in simple—but grand—holiday arrangements.

The room with a mantel is a privileged one; it has a natural focal point and gathering area. But even rooms without mantels can be decorated using the ideas found in this chapter. Simply substitute another area to set the stage. A sideboard, a hutch, a single shelf, or a long side table can serve as the room's architectural focal point and exhibition area.

Another decorating approach is to select individual elements from these featured groupings, such as the Embossed Velvet Frames or the Hand-dipped Candles, to develop subtle points of interest in different areas of a room, instead of making an entire decorative landscape.

"The Mantel" is rich with fast and easy ideas that provide dramatic results. With a simple array of greens, fruit, and candles, you can transform a room's atmosphere in an instant. A collection of Gold Candlesticks can create a strong, visual impact and a new fabric dying technique will allow you to make contemporary velvet stockings in brilliant colors.

Adapt these fabulous projects to achieve any effect you wish: incorporate a few distinctive details into your current mantel treatment, or try a new and elaborate festive look in some other interior space of your home.

Dyed Velvet Stockings

OF COURSE, STOCKINGS DON'T HAVE TO BE RED! THIS FOOLPROOF DYEING TECHNIQUE IS A FUN, FRESH WAY TO CREATE BEAUTIFUL VELVET CHRISTMAS STOCKINGS IN MANY UNIQUE COLORS. BELOW ARE DIRECTIONS FOR DYEING FOUR YARDS OF VELVET IN THE COLORS PICTURED HERE. USE YOUR OWN FAVORITE PATTERN TO CREATE THE STOCKINGS AND EXPERIMENT WITH OTHER DYE COLORS IF YOU WISH.

TIME REQUIRED: 2 HOURS FOR DYEING; 1 DAY FOR DRYING

MATERIALS NEEDED

Newspaper

2 plastic drop cloths (or plastic garbage bags)

Paper towels

Masking tape

Permanent marker

4 plastic spray bottles

Scissors

4 yards of white cotton velvet

Rubber gloves

1 package Tinfix fabric dye in following colors:

# 71 Meadow Green	# 15 Orange Vif
# 60 Vert Celedon	# 30 Tyrian Rose

Sponge

Clip-style pant hangers

DIRECTIONS FOR DYEING

STEP 1 Protect work surface with newspaper covered with plastic drop cloth. Tape down drop cloth edges.

STEP 2 Set up second area for drying. Cover floor with second drop cloth; cover with paper towels to absorb draining water from velvet.

STEP 3 Make masking tape label for each spray bottle to indicate dye color.

STEP 4 Cut velvet into four 1-yard pieces.

STEP 5 Take one yard of fabric and cut out four 1-inch squares from a corner for color testing.

STEP 6 Saturate all velvet with water; squeeze out excess. Set aside.

STEP 7 Fill a spray bottle halfway with water; put on rubber gloves. Add 1 teaspoon of Meadow Green dye; close bottle and shake vigorously to mix.

STEP 8 Spray a test square with color. If it looks too light, add dye in ½ teaspoons until desired color is reached; if it looks too dark, add more water to bottle as necessary.

STEP 9 Lay one saturated yard of velvet onto drop cloth. Spray fabric with dye until evenly colored. Move fabric to drying area and place on top of paper towels to dry.

STEP 10 Repeat Steps 7 through 9 for remaining colors. Be sure to sponge down drop cloth between colors to remove traces of previous dye. Change plastic if necessary.

STEP 11 Change saturated paper towels under velvet every two hours, or as needed. Once velvet is no longer dripping, remove from plastic and hang to dry using pant hangers in drying room or bathroom.

Note: Once completely dry, follow steps for creating stockings using your pattern. Each yard of velvet used, will yield 1 stocking. Adjust your fabric needs to the pattern if necessary.

Fresh Fruit and Foliage Arrangement

THE QUICK AND EASY BINDING TECHNIQUE ALLOWS YOU TO MAKE A SPECTACULAR ARRANGEMENT IN ANY SIZE.

The Garland

WITH THE SIMPLE AND QUICK BINDING OF LEMON LEAF STEMS, YOU HAVE THE BEGINNING OF A BEAUTIFUL ARRANGEMENT.

TIME REQUIRED: 1 ½ HOURS

MATERIALS NEEDED FOR 4-FOOT GARLAND

30 stems lemon leaves (approximately 2 bunches)

Green florist wire

Scissors

DIRECTIONS

STEP 1   Pick through lemon leaves to separate out the 30 best leaves.

STEP 2   Hold 2 stems with left hand, stems pointing to the right. Holding florist wire in right hand, wrap wire around stems 2-3 times to secure. Do not cut wire. Position a third stem with the others, with stem also pointing right, but further down so that leaves partially cover first 2 stems. Fasten third stem to others by wrapping with wire.

STEP 3   Continue adding 1 or 2 stems at a time in same fashion until you achieve desired length. Cut wire and secure end around stem. (Make garland slightly longer than mantel so it will hang over the edges.)

Sugared Fruit

ORDINARY LEMONS AND LIMES BECOME
EXTRAORDINARY WHEN COATED WITH THIS
GLIMMERING LAYER OF SUGAR.

TIME REQUIRED: 1 HOUR

MATERIALS NEEDED FOR
SUGARED FRUIT

Aluminum foil

Granulated sugar

2 bowls

2 eggs

Sponge brush

4 lemons

4 limes

DIRECTIONS

STEP 1   Protect work surface with aluminum foil.

STEP 2   Pour sugar into one bowl and set aside. Separate eggs, placing whites in other bowl. Dispose of yolks.

STEP 3   Use sponge brush to paint lemon with egg white. Roll painted lemon in bowl of sugar to coat. Place on foil to dry. Repeat for remaining lemons and limes. Sugared fruit may be handled within ½ hour, but overnight drying will enhance frosted effect.

ASSEMBLING MANTEL
ARRANGEMENT:

STEP 1   Position garland (see pages 32-33) on mantel so that ends drape over each side. Bend some stems to hang over front of mantel.

STEP 2   Add Hand-dipped Candles (see page 37) by placing them in front and behind garland so that leaves weave in and out around them.

STEP 3   Place lemons and limes alone and in small clusters at base of candles. Sugared coating will reflect light from candles.

Hand-dipped Candles

THIS IS A TERRIFIC WAY TO RECYCLE CANDLE STUBS. JUST MELT THE STUBS OF ANY OLD CANDLES AND USE IT AS DIPPING BATH FOR PLAIN CANDLES. HERE, WHITE- AND CREAM-COLORED CANDLES ARE DIPPED IN THE MELTED WAX OF OLD DARK GREEN AND YELLOW CANDLES. THE RESULTS ARE PERFECTLY COLORED LIME GREEN AND SUNSHINE YELLOW CANDLES TO ACCENT THE LEMON LEAF MANTEL GARLAND.

TIME REQUIRED: 1 HOUR

MATERIALS NEEDED
Aluminum foil
Inexpensive, large, shallow frying pan
Colored candle stubs
Rubber gloves
Metal tongs with plastic or wooden handle
White- or cream-colored candles

DIRECTIONS

STEP 1   Protect work surface with aluminum foil.

STEP 2   Line pan with foil. Add candle stubs of the same color and place over burner on low heat. Put on rubber gloves for protection.

STEP 3   Rotate candles with tongs as they melt. Use tongs to remove wicks as wax becomes liquid.

STEP 4   Holding white- or cream-colored candle horizontally with one hand on each end, roll in colored wax to coat. Repeated rolling will deepen color. Note: Avoid resting the candle on the bottom of the frying pan or it will melt.

STEP 5   When satisfied with depth of color, stand candle on foil or place in foil-lined candle holder. Repeat Step 4 for additional candles in same color.

STEP 6   Repeat Steps 2 through 4 for next color. Note: if any wax has gotten on frying pan, it can be removed by boiling some water in pan. Wax will melt and float to surface of water. Pour out wax and water.

Other ideas: Spoon wax over portions of candle to create a marbleized effect or use different colored waxes for a multi-colored look.

Embossed Velvet Frames

PRINT VELVET WITH UNIQUE DESIGNS AND USE IT TO MAKE THESE PLUSH, DECORATIVE FRAMES. LINE THEM UP ON YOUR MANTEL FILLED WITH PHOTOGRAPHS OF YOUR FAMILY AND FRIENDS, OR GIVE THEM AS HOLIDAY GIFTS.

TIME REQUIRED: 1 HOUR PER FRAME

MATERIALS NEEDED
Iron and ironing board
1 yard of red velvet (enough for six 6 ½ x 8-inch frames
and two 6 ½ x 12 ½-inch frames)
8 frames of the above dimensions
Pencil
Ruler
Scissors
Wire cutters
Armature wire
Pliers
Spray starch
Newspaper
Spray adhesive

DIRECTIONS

STEP 1   Iron velvet on medium setting on the wrong side to smooth any wrinkles. Lay velvet out on flat work surface, wrong side up.

STEP 2   For each frame, trace outline with pencil on velvet by increasing the frame dimensions 2 inches on each side, for example, for 6 ½ x 8-inch frame, draw 8 ½ x 10-inch rectangle. Cut out marked rectangles.

STEP 3   With center glass removed, center frame on velvet to trace outside and inside of frame. Remove frame. Use pencil and ruler to draw additional rectangle ¼-inch smaller than inside rectangle. Beginning with one outside corner of velvet, draw a diagonal line connecting the corner to corresponding frame corner. Draw a second line that is perpendicular to diagonal line ¼-inch outside the frame corner. Cut along perpendicular line to eliminate outside corner of the fabric. Repeat at each corner. Repeat entire step for remaining frames. Set velvet aside.

STEP 4 To make the patterns for embossing, use wire cutters to cut a 6-inch length of armature wire for a circle, a 3-inch piece for a triangle, and a 5-length for a star.

STEP 5 To make circular swirl design, hold one end of 6-inch wire with pliers. Using fingers, wind other end of wire around center until shape forms. Use pliers and fingers to bend other wires into star and triangle patterns.

STEP 6 Set iron to hottest setting. Place the wire pattern on ironing board; referring to pencil outlines, position frame area of velvet, wrong side up, on top of wire. Spray velvet with starch over wire pattern. Press iron (no steam) onto velvet firmly; hold for 10 seconds. Repeat to cover all frame areas of velvet with embossed patterns.

STEP 7 In a well-ventilated area, place one rectangle of embossed velvet, wrong side up, onto newspaper-covered work surface.

STEP 8 Spray velvet with adhesive following manufacturer's instructions. Using pencil outlines as a guide, quickly lay frame face down in center of fabric. Immediately smooth out wrinkles and bubbles. If needed, peel back fabric and quickly reapply it.

STEP 9 At each outside corner, fold the ¼-inch of fabric over corner. Then, fold sides as you would when wrapping a gift, and fold down each flap, starting at top side. Smooth with hands to adhere.

STEP 10 Using scissors, cut hole in center of velvet and cut away smallest interior rectangle. Looking at front side of frame, snip remaining inside corners of velvet to edge of inside frame corner.

STEP 11 Wrap remaining ¼-inch of fabric around inside of frame; press firmly to adhere. Trim away any excess fabric on backside of frame. Allow adhesive to set 20 minutes. Repeat beginning at Step 7 for remaining frames.

STEP 12 To complete frames, reinsert glass, add picture, and replace backing. (Many frames also include extra cardboard to secure photograph in place. Velvet lining may negate need for this piece.)

Gold Candlesticks

TRANSFORM MISMATCHED WOODEN CANDLESTICKS INTO A LUSTROUS COORDINATED SET FOR ANY DISPLAY; A FEW LIGHT COATS OF GOLD PAINT UNIFY THE SET BY ADDING A GLOWING PATINA.

TIME REQUIRED: 30 MINUTES PLUS OVERNIGHT DRYING

MATERIALS NEEDED

3 wooden candlesticks
(pictured here: 10-, 14-, and 18-inch candlesticks)
Fine grit sandpaper
Cotton rag
Cardboard box (same height as candlesticks)
Utility knife
Newspaper
Rubber gloves
Disposable face mask
8-ounce can gold spray paint
Acrylic spray sealer (optional)

DIRECTIONS

STEP 1   Smooth surface of wood on candlestick using fine sandpaper; wipe away dust with damp rag.

STEP 2   Cut away top and two adjacent sides from cardboard box using utility knife. Line box bottom with newspaper and position candlesticks in center area.

STEP 3   Slip on rubber gloves and face mask. In well-ventilated area and following spray-paint manufacturer's instructions, spray all surfaces of candlesticks, using circular motion. Be sure to spray between carved details and rims; let dry for a few minutes.

STEP 4   Apply second coat of paint, as in Step 3. Let dry overnight.

Optional: Coat painted surface with acrylic spray sealer.

White Rose Arrangement

THIS LUSH, VOLUMINOUS FLORAL ARRANGEMENT IS EASY TO MAKE BY ADDING WHITE SILK ROSES TO A GENEROUS FIELD OF IVY. YOU CAN ADAPT THIS ARRANGEMENT TO OTHER SEASONS BY CHANGING THE COLOR OF THE ACCENT FABRIC OR BY ADDING DIFFERENT VARIETIES OF FLOWERS.

TIME REQUIRED: 1 HOUR

MATERIALS NEEDED

4 blocks floral foam (9 x 3 x 4-inch)

4 shallow aluminum pans

(the floral blocks will need to fit inside them)

4 bricks or wooden blocks

Packing tape

2 bunches of bushy ivy

(approximately 15 stems per bunch)

2 bunches of variegated bushy ivy

(approximately 15 stems per bunch)

Scissors

18 white silk roses

3 yards mauve silk moiré fabric

DIRECTIONS

STEP 1   Soak floral foam with water in sink. Allow excess water to drain off.

STEP 2   Line up aluminum pans and center on mantel.

STEP 3   To weight arrangement, attach each foam block to brick (or wooden block). Stack and then wrap packing tape around one brick and foam block 6 or 7 times. (Tape will not adhere to foam, but will secure.) Repeat for each foam block. Place weighted foam blocks into pans, foam side up.

STEP 4   Press stems of plain and variegated ivy into foam blocks, alternating varieties as you go. Add ivy until base and pans are entirely covered. (To poke stems through tape-covered areas of foam, puncture tape with scissors.)

STEP 5   Insert roses into foam, one by one, spaced evenly throughout arrangement.

STEP 6   For finishing touch, drape silk moiré around arrangement. Slide one edge of fabric under pans to secure. Allow center to swoop downward, with sides draping up over sides of mantel. Outside corners can be tucked under bricks to secure. Tuck raw edges of fabric into folds. Arrangement should last 1 to 2 weeks.

Vine and Grape Wreath

THIS PRETTY DECORATION WILL INSPIRE YOU TO COMBINE LEFTOVER CRAFT AND FLORAL MATERIALS WITH NATURAL ELEMENTS FOUND IN SURROUNDING LANDSCAPE. ATTACH SINGLE PINECONES, SEED PODS AND BERRIES TO A SIMPLE VINE BASE.

TIME REQUIRED: 1 HOUR

MATERIALS NEEDED
Hot glue gun and glue sticks
20 silk berry stems (pictured here: leafy blueberry, currant, raspberry, and blackberry)
8-inch-diameter vine wreath
4 grape clusters
Medium-gauge wire
Wire cutters
10 sprigs: eucalyptus, ivy, or other greens, as desired
4 stems white statice
10-12 assorted silk leaves
4 pine cones, sprayed gold

DIRECTIONS

STEP 1   Using a clock orientation, use hot-glue to insert and adhere ends of berry stems in vines of wreath, mixing types and decorating each side of wreath separately as follows: At 8 o'clock, insert stems with berries radiating outward; repeat at 4 o'clock position, until all decoration meets at 12 o'clock.

STEP 2   Add grape clusters at 11 o'clock and 1 o'clock, using wire to secure, if necessary.

STEP 3   Continue filling in sections using sprigs, white statice, and leaves, using hot glue to secure.

STEP 4   Make stems for pine cones by wrapping 8-inch-length of wire under top petals, twisting ends of wire to secure. Position cone at top section of wreath, inserting wire stem between decoration and vines, securing at back; repeat for remaining cones.

STEP 5   Stand back from wreath and assess decoration, hot-gluing additional leaves in bare spots, as necessary. Let dry.

the table

4

Cocktail parties, intimate dinners, and late-night desserts are what make the holidays feel like the holidays. On these festive occasions, a beautiful table enhances the warm welcome we extend. The table is the glorious gathering place where family and friends come together to partake in the rituals of eating, drinking, and sharing, and where special decorations can be seen at close glance.

From eye-catching centerpieces to silky and lush tablecloths and runners, the easy-to-follow projects in this chapter will carry a special note of cheer to all the season's celebrations. The Embossed Velvet Table Runner and Napkin Pocket will transform any table into a sophisticated stage for entertaining. Plain red velvet is embossed with a beautiful pattern using the simplest tools—a metal trivet and an iron. The Evergreen Wreath Centerpiece is a lovely complement to this matching velvet set.

The soft, green Organdy Tablecloth is an unpredictable and splendid departure from typical holiday table treatments. Each corner is accented with a beautiful bouquet of organdy roses, easily made by folding a piece of ribbon into triangles.

In "The Table," discover an attractive new way to wrap wines and spirits, as well as the simple art of glass etching, a frosting technique that can be used to decorate any glass object. These ideas will enhance all of your holiday entertaining for years to come.

Velvet Leaf Wreath

THIS SIMPLE WREATH WILL ADD COLOR AND SPARKLE TO ANY TABLE AS A CENTERPIECE OR AS A
FESTIVE DECORATION FOR A CHAIRBACK, DOORKNOB, OR BED POST.

TIME REQUIRED: 1 HOUR

MATERIALS NEEDED

Newspaper

Fresh or silk leaf (for pattern)

Bristol paper

Pencil

Spray adhesive

Velvet scraps: light blue, dark blue, and lavender

Scissors

Silver leaf foil

Permanent marker

Wax paper

Masking tape

½ yard light blue organza

Pearlized white fabric paint

10-inch-diameter vine wreath

Hot glue gun and glue sticks

1 ½-inch miniature plastic and flocked peaches

7 silver ball ornaments, 1 ½-inch-diameter

Ribbon

DIRECTIONS:

STEP 1   Protect work surface with newspaper.

STEP 2   To make leaf pattern, lay fresh leaf on bristol paper
and trace around perimeter, using pencil; cut out leaf.

STEP 3   Lay bristol paper leaf on work surface and coat with
spray adhesive following manufacturer's directions. Position
velvet scrap on paper and smooth velvet flat, using hands. Cut
away any velvet that extends beyond leaf pattern.

STEP 4   Repeat Steps 2 and 3 to create 6 light blue leaves, 2
dark blue leaves, and 2 lavender leaves.

STEP 5   Lay leaf velvet-side down. Apply spray adhesive and
place piece of silver leaf over bristol paper; smooth down with
your hands until no paper is left exposed.

STEP 6   Repeat Step 5 for the remaining 9 leaves. To shape
leaves, fold in half lengthwise and secure crease by pinching
with fingers.

STEP 7   To make organza leaf, trace another leaf pattern with
black marker. Lay sheet of wax paper on flat work surface and
slip template under wax paper. Lay organza over template,
taping sides to secure. Trace around lines, using fabric paint; let
dry completely.

STEP 8   Peel fabric away from wax paper. Use scissors to cut
out each leaf, cutting around edge of extruded paint; set aside.

STEP 9   Repeat Steps 7 and 8 to make 5 more leaves.

STEP 10 To decorate wreath, use hot glue to secure one end
of each leaf, positioning as in photograph or as desired. Use
hot glue to secure fruit and silver balls, as desired, interspers-
ing fruit and balls in leaves.

STEP 11 Use as centerpiece or tie a ribbon around the top to
hang as wreath.

Embossed Velvet Table Runner and Napkin Pockets

MAKE A LUXURIOUS RED VELVET RUNNER WITH MATCHING NAPKIN POCKETS, USING AN EASY EMBOSSING TECHNIQUE AND SIMPLE SEWING PROCESS.

Table Runner

TIME REQUIRED: 1 HOUR

Runner finished size: 16 x 54 inches

MATERIALS NEEDED FOR BOTH PROJECTS

2 yards red rayon velvet

Scissors

Ruler and pencil

4 x 4-inch decorative metal trivet (for embossing pattern)

Iron and ironing board

Spray starch

Straight pins

4 5-inch-long tassels

Sewing machine

Red thread to match

Needle

DIRECTIONS

STEP 1   Cut two 17 x 55-inch rectangles of velvet. Set one aside.

STEP 2   Lay one piece of velvet on flat work surface, wrong side up.

STEP 3   Place trivet at one corner, leaving 1-inch border at each edge of fabric. Use pencil to draw outline of border around trivet. Move trivet down long edge of fabric marking outlines as you go. Leave 4 inches of space between each trivet square. Repeat along opposite long edge of fabric.

STEP 4   To emboss velvet pattern, place velvet on ironing board, wrong side up. Slide trivet under one marked square, matching corners. Spray marked square of velvet with starch. Position hot iron (no steam) over marked area and press iron onto velvet firmly; hold for 10 seconds. Lift and reposition iron until entire trivet has been pressed. Avoid shifting position of velvet over trivet. Repeat this step to emboss trivet pattern along each edge.

STEP 5   Place the other velvet rectangle on flat work surface, right side up.

STEP 6   Pin top threads of tassel to corner of rectangle, with lower ends of tassel lying toward center of rectangle; repeat to pin tassle at each corner.

STEP 7   Position and pin second rectangle of velvet over first, right sides together, raw edges even.

STEP 8   Using sewing machine, stitch ½-inch seam around outside edges, leaving 7-inch opening for turning. Make sure tassels remain properly positioned at corners.

STEP 9   Clip excess fabric from corners, remove pins, and turn to right side, flattening seams and making neat corners.

STEP 10 Turn in remaining edges and hand-stitch closed.

Napkin Pockets

TIME REQUIRED: 1 HOUR

Napkin Pocket finished size: 4 x 5 inches
(Yield: 4 napkin pockets)

DIRECTIONS

STEP 1   Measure and cut one 12 x 5-inch rectangle.

STEP 2   Lay velvet wrong side up on work surface and place the trivet in center of right half of the rectangle. Trace outline of trivet with pencil.

STEP 3   Follow Step 4 from runner directions to emboss velvet.

STEP 4   Fold rectangle in half, right sides together, so that folded edge is at the bottom. At each top edge, opposite fold, make a 1-inch hem and machine-stich.

STEP 5   Pin sides together and machine-stitch ½-inch seam on raw edges.

STEP 6   Clip corners, remove pins, and trim loose threads. Turn to right side.

STEP 7   Repeat Steps 1 through 6 to complete remaining napkin pockets.

Evergreen Wreath Centerpiece

THIS LUSH, TRADITIONAL EVERGREEN WREATH WILL
COMPLEMENT ANY TABLE SETTING. THE BOUGHS
WILL RELEASE A WONDERFUL PINE AROMA WHILE
THE CANDLES WILL ADD A SOFT GLOW.

TIME REQUIRED: 1 ½ HOURS

MATERIALS NEEDED FOR THE WREATH
18-inch ring with molded plastic base and Styrofoam inset
Pruning shears
15 fresh evergreen boughs
(you can use cuttings from your tree)

MATERIALS NEEDED FOR CANDLE SPRAY
12 stems artificial berries
12 stems artificial leafy branches
Medium-gauge florist wire
Wire cutters
12 pine cones sprayed gold
8 red glass ornaments, 2-inch diameter
4 candles, 10-inch length
12 wooden skewers

DIRECTIONS FOR THE WREATH

STEP 1   Soak foam ring in water.

STEP 2   Use shears to cut evergreen branch into 6- and 8-inch lengths.

STEP 3   Insert stems into foam, one at a time, until foam is concealed, alternating lengths and thicknesses for natural look; set aside.

DIRECTIONS FOR THE CANDLE SPRAYS

STEP 1   Gather 4 stems each of artificial berries and leafy branches and arrange into soft spray.

STEP 2   Bind spray together with wire just below leafy section.

STEP 3   Use wire cutters to cut all stems even, 3 inches below binding.

STEP 4   Add 3 gold pine cones to spray by wrapping them together with wire, then twisting the wire around the back of spray binding.

STEP 5   Again, using wire, attach 2 ornaments to spray.

STEP 6   Repeat Steps 1 through 5 to make 3 more sprays.

STEP 7   Insert sprays into foam, evenly spaced at each quarter.

STEP 8   Measure candle spikes by inserting skewer into wreath near spray; push down until skewer touches plastic wreath mold; mark skewer 2 inches higher than spray. Remove and cut skewer at mark. Cut 3 skewers for each candle, or 12 altogether.

STEP 9   Position 3 skewers against bottom of candle, allowing 2 inches to extend against sides of candle; secure by wrapping with wire. Repeat to make 3 candle spikes.

STEP 10 Position and insert 1 candle at each spray. Finished diameter of centerpiece is 24 inches.

Organdy Tablecloth

THIS SHIMMERING, GLAMOROUS TABLECLOTH IS COMPRISED OF TWO LAYERS, A SHEER WHITE LAYER WHICH COVERS A PLAIN WHITE TABLE CLOTH, AND THE GREEN OVERLAY, WHICH IS TRIMMED IN WHITE AND ACCENTED WITH A BOUQUET OF RIBBON ROSES.

TIME REQUIRED: 2 ½ HOURS

MATERIALS NEEDED FOR GREEN ORGANDY OVERLAY

12 yards (72-inch-wide) green organdy
Iron and ironing board
Straight pins
Scissors
Thread to match green organdy
Sewing machine
5 yards 2-inch-wide white organdy ribbon

MATERIALS NEEDED FOR RIBBON ROSES

2 ½-inch-wide organdy wire-edged ribbon
(4 yards each of the following colors: white, eggplant, burgundy, light green, and hunter green)
Needle
Thread to match green organdy

MATERIALS NEEDED FOR WHITE ORGANDY TABLECLOTH

4 yards of white organdy
White thread

DIRECTIONS FOR GREEN ORGANDY OVERLAY

STEP 1   Iron green organdy on light setting.

STEP 2   Fold green organdy in half with wrong sides touching, placing cut edges together. Pin along three cut edges and press folded edge. Trim all loose threads.

STEP 3   Using green thread, machine-stitch ¼-inch seam around 4 sides.

STEP 4   Press 2-inch-wide organdy white ribbon in half lengthwise. With fabric spread flat and starting at one corner, wrap organdy ribbon around outside edges, pinning as you go. Half of ribbon should cover front side of fabric, and half should cover back. At corners, tuck excess fabric into triangular crease and pin down.

STEP 5   After final edge is covered, cut ribbon 1 inch beyond corner. Fold extending fabric toward back and pin down. (Corner will be covered by roses.)

STEP 6   Attach ribbon to green organdy by machine stitching a seam ⅛-inch from edge of white organdy ribbon all around. Set aside.

STEP 1   Cut the white, eggplant, and burgundy wire-edged ribbons into four 1-yard lengths for each.

STEP 2   Place a 1-yard piece of white wire-edged ribbon on work surface horizontally. Place index finger of left hand on the center of ribbon. With right hand, take length of ribbon on right, raise it, then lay it down directly south creating a corner fold. Ribbon length on right should be on top. If ribbons were hands of a clock, right hand would be at 6 o'clock, and left hand ribbon at 9 o'clock.

STEP 3   Holding ribbon in same position, pick it up, holding center. (Throughout entire process, always hold center of ribbon while folding.) Take ribbon at 6 o'clock and move it to 12 o'clock, going behind center fold. Then take ribbon at 9 o'clock and move to 3 o'clock, again going behind center fold.

STEP 4   Continue folding ribbons behind center, alternating first ribbon between 6 o'clock and 12 o'clock, and second ribbon between 9 o'clock and 3 o'clock, until you have one inch of each ribbon remaining.

STEP 5   Place two ends together; holding them tightly, release center folds. Ribbon will pop out and look like a long accordion. (Don't let go of ends.)

STEP 6   Take one ribbon end and slowly slide it downward along other side of ribbon. Rose will begin to form. Stop when ribbon rose forms. (You have gone too far if it starts collapsing on itself.)

STEP 7   Bind ends of ribbon together by wrapping thread around them and tying a knot to secure.

STEP 8   Leave 1-inch ribbon as stem, then trim excess.

STEP 9   Using your fingers, shape wire edged ribbon as needed to articulate rose petals.

STEP 10   Repeat Steps 2 through 9 with remaining pieces of ribbon.

STEP 11   Bind together 1 white, 1 eggplant, and 1 burgundy rose with thread to make a bouquet. Repeat with remaining roses to make 3 more bouquets.

STEP 12   To make bows, cut light green and hunter green ribbons each into four 1-yard pieces. Take one piece of light green ribbon and bend to create 3 loops. Bind together with thread. Repeat for remaining 3 pieces of light green ribbon.

STEP 13   Take one piece of the hunter green wire edged ribbon and tie into bow. Repeat for remaining three pieces.

STEP 14   Using needle and thread, stitch one hunter green bow to back of one bouquet. Stitch light green bow to back of hunter green bow. Repeat for remaining 3 bouquets.

DIRECTIONS FOR ASSEMBLY

Using needle and thread, sew one completed bouquet to each corner of green organdy overlay. Attach the bouquets at several points so that they hang flat, stabilized against the green organdy. (You will need to move the roses and shape them so that the stems don't show.)

DIRECTIONS FOR WHITE ORGANDY TABLECLOTH

STEP 1   Cut 4 yards of white organdy in half to get two 2-yard lengths.

STEP 2   Pin 2 of the edges together and sew the 2 pieces together with your sewing machine. You should have one large square.

STEP 3   Iron the seam flat and pin a ¼-inch hem around all 4 outside edges. Sew the hem down to create finished edges. Iron flat.

A Partridge in a Pear Tree Topiary

ONE GLITTERING PARTRIDGE IS NESTLED BETWEEN THE BRANCHES OF A TOPIARY AND SPARKLING PEARS ACCENT THE VARIEGATED FOLIAGE. MADE IN A MINATURE SIZE, THIS TOPIARY IS A WELCOME ADDITION AT ANY PLACE SETTING.

TIME REQUIRED: 1 HOUR

MATERIALS NEEDED FOR TOPIARY
Newspaper
Florist foam, large enough to fill container
Silver container for base, 2-5 inches high with 2-5-inch diameter (pictured here: a 2 ½ x 5-inch candy dish)
Scissors
1 bunch fresh variegated pit
Floral tape
20 silk leaves with center wire, each ½-inch long

DIRECTIONS FOR TOPIARY

STEP 1   Protect work surface with newspaper.

STEP 2   Place floral foam in the center of the newspaper. Hold silver container upside down and lower over center of foam. Press container down to fill with foam.

STEP 3   Use scissors to carefully trim away excess foam from top and sides of container. Add water to foam and set aside.

STEP 4   Gather 4-5 stems of variegated pit. Wrap stems together with floral tape to form a shape resembling a small tree.

STEP 5   Push wrapped stems into center of floral foam. Cover exposed foam surface with small silk leaves by pushing wire stems ends into foam. Set aside.

MATERIALS NEEDED FOR PEARS AND PARTRIDGE

Aluminum foil

5 plastic-coated Styrofoam pears

Aleene's Tacky Thin-bodied Glue

Sponge brush

11-gram container of gold glitter

11-gram container of lime green glitter

3-5 inch-long plastic bird with wire stem

144 3 mm magenta rhinestones

144 6 mm magenta rhinestones

Green thread

DIRECTIONS FOR PARTRIDGE

STEP 1   Coat plastic bird with glue using sponge brush. Sprinkle bird with gold glitter until covered and allow to dry.

STEP 2   Apply additional glue around beak and head and begin to layer 3 mm rhinestones over bird.

STEP 3   Continue adding glue and rhinestones to sections, moving from head toward tail. Use 6 mm rhinestones for wings and breast.

STEP 4   When bird is completely covered, set aside to dry.

DIRECTIONS FOR PEARS

STEP 1   Protect work surface with aluminum foil.

STEP 2   Coat one pear with glue using sponge brush. Sprinkle gold glitter over pear until completely covered. Allow to dry 5 minutes.

STEP 3   Apply additional glue in vertical strip over one quarter of the pear. Sprinkle lime green glitter over glue-coated section to create accent.

STEP 4   Repeat Steps 2 and 3 for remaining pears. Place pears on aluminum foil to dry.

ASSEMBLING TOPIARY

STEP 1   Cut five 3-inch pieces of thread.

STEP 2   Tie one piece of thread into a knot around stem of one pear, with length of thread even on both sides. Tie free ends into knot to form loop. Repeat for remaining pears.

STEP 3   Position partridge in center of topiary by twisting wire stem around supportive branch. Add pears to surround topiary by looping them over various branches to create the finished project.

Frosted Grape Centerpiece

COAT DIFFERENT VARIETIES OF GRAPES WITH SUGAR AND
ASSEMBLE THIS STYLISH AND EDIBLE CENTERPIECE.

TIME REQUIRED: ½ HOUR

MATERIALS NEEDED:

1 egg

Large bowl

3 fresh, well shaped bunches of grapes

Aluminum baking sheet

Silk grape leaves

1 sponge brush

Granulated sugar

DIRECTIONS

STEP 1   Separate egg, placing the white in bowl. Dispose of yolk.

STEP 2   Place grapes on the aluminum baking sheet.

STEP 3   Use sponge brush to paint grapes with egg white.

STEP 4   Holding one bunch of grapes by stem, pour granulated sugar
over grapes, turning grapes as you pour to ensure proper coverage.

STEP 5   Repeat Steps 3 and 4 to frost remaining bunches of grapes.

STEP 6   Set all bunches on baking sheet. Brush silk grape leaves with
egg white.

STEP 7   Dip leaves in granulated sugar and add to baking sheet.

STEP 8   Place baking sheet in refrigerator. The frosting will be set in as little as half an hour, but effect will improve if left overnight.

STEP 9   To serve, arrange frosted grapes on serving dish. Add frosted silk
leaves at the tops of each bunch as garnish, if desired.

Gift-wrapped Wine Bottles

THE EXOTIC TEXTURE AND BEAUTIFUL COLORS OF RICE PAPER MAKE IT THE PERFECT WRAPPING FOR BOTTLES OF WINE FOR YOUR TABLE OR GIFT-GIVING. RICE PAPER IS AS PLIABLE AND EASY TO WORK WITH AS TISSUE PAPER.

TIME REQUIRED: 15 MINUTES PER BOTTLE

MATERIALS NEEDED

1 25 x 38-inch sheet of banana chip rice paper

Hot glue gun and glue sticks

Scissors

1 yard of decorative trim (ribbon, sequins, cording)

DIRECTIONS:

STEP 1   Set the wine bottle in the center of the rice paper. Pull the paper up around the sides of the bottle, wrapping the "winged" sides toward the back of the bottle.

STEP 2   Crease the excess paper into repeating ½-inch folds towards the bottle to create a finished seam. Secure the seam against the bottle using hot glue.

STEP 3   Twist the paper at the neck of the bottle and bend the excess paper over the top of the bottle and down the backside. Secure the paper to the neck using hot glue.

STEP 4   Cut one piece of desired trim in half. Attach one end to the back seam over the neck of the bottle. Wrap the trim around the neck 3-4 times and attach other end to back seam with hot glue, trimming any excess.

STEP 5   Wrap trim around base of bottle as in Step 4.

Etched Votive Candleholders

ETCHING LETTERS ONTO SMALL GLASS VOTIVES GIVES YOU ENDLESS POSSIBILITIES FOR CREATING ANY HOLIDAY MESSAGE. STACK OR LINE UP ETCHED VOTIVES ON A TABLE, OR MONOGRAM ONE FOR EACH GUEST TO TAKE HOME AS A SPECIAL KEEPSAKE OF THE EVENING.

TIME REQUIRED: 1 HOUR

MATERIALS NEEDED:

Etching cream

Aluminum foil

4 green glass votive candle holders

1 package ½-inch vinyl self-adhesive letters

Rubber gloves

Sponge brush

4 white votive candles

DIRECTIONS

STEP 1   Read manufacturer's instructions for the brand of etching cream you select. Note special handling and timing requirements.

STEP 2   Protect work surface with aluminum foil. Place clean glass votives on aluminum foil.

STEP 3   Apply letter "N" sheet to center of one holder. Press down firmly with fingers. Add square "dot" from lower case "I" to each side of "N" (see photo for placement).

STEP 4   Repeat Step 3 for remaining "O," "E," and "L."

STEP 5   Wearing rubber gloves, open etching cream. Starting with one holder, use sponge brush to apply thick coat of etching cream to cover entire exterior surface. You may brush cream right over vinyl letters. Repeat for remaining holders. Close etching cream container and rinse brush.

STEP 6   After recommended etching period passes, rinse off etching cream with tap water. Rub at glass or use sponge brush to ensure that all etching cream is rinsed away from crevices. Pat votives dry and peel off letters. Place the votive candles inside, then line up on the table.

the tree

*T*he tree is the symbolic heart of the holiday home, the center stage around which the holiday celebration takes place. Decorating the tree is an activity for which no rules exist—except to turn it into something beautiful.

"The Tree" contains fabulous new ways of reinventing the old, like an antiquing method for the Antiqued Treetop Star, easy instructions for making retro Miniature Beaded Fruit, and a lovely design for sparkling Glitterball Ornaments.

There are also several unique ideas for turning simple, round glass ornaments into something special. You can treat the insides with paint, the outsides with metallic tape, or glue several together to make tiered sculptures. Add beads, rhinestones, silk leaves or gold bullion for even more decorative ideas.

You'll also find an inexpensive technique for making attractive Wire Mesh Mini Lights that will provide the perfect illumination for the tree; the lights will cast a warm glow through the metallic weave.

There are enough decorations in this chapter to trim the entire tree from top to bottom, with projects suitable for every member of the family. It is fun to create a tradition of decorating the tree with unique and beautiful decorations, made in your own home, which will be treasured by all and used year after year.

White Chocolate and Sprinkle Wreaths

HANG THESE SNOW WHITE CHOCOLATE WREATHS, COATED WITH BRIGHTLY COLORED
SPRINKLES ON YOUR TREE. CHILDREN WILL HAVE AS MUCH FUN EATING THEM AS THEY
WILL IN MAKING THEM.

TIME REQUIRED: ½ HOUR

YIELD

Makes about 30 rings, about 1 ½ inches wide

MATERIALS NEEDED

Baking sheet

Parchment paper

8 ounces white chocolate

¾ teaspoon vegetable shortening

Double boiler

Pastry bag with ¼-inch tip

Nonpareil sprinkles

Scissors

3 ½ yards gold cord

DIRECTIONS

STEP 1   Cover baking sheet with sheet of parchment paper.
Set aside.

STEP 2   Heat chocolate and shortening together in top of
double boiler, stirring until melted.

STEP 3   Remove from stove and spoon half of chocolate mixture into pastry bag with ¼-inch round tip. Working fairly
quickly to avoid hardening of chocolate, push mixture toward
bottom of bag and twist top of pastry bag.

STEP 4   Squeeze out chocolate mixture into rings onto parchment paper. Add nonpareil sprinkles to rings while still warm.

STEP 5   Warm up remaining chocolate on double boiler and
repeat Steps 3 and 4.

STEP 6   Place baking sheet in refrigerator to cool. Mean-
while, cut gold cord into 4-inch pieces.

STEP 7   Once chocolate has cooled, remove from refrigerator. Slip one piece of gold cord through center of each wreath;
tie a knot at top to form a loop for hanging.

Tiered Ball Ornaments

CREATE FANCIFUL TIERED ORNAMENTS BY
STACKING AND GLUING BALL ORNAMENTS
TOGETHER. YOU CAN EXPERIMENT BY ATTACHING
ORNAMENTS OF DIFFERENT COLORS AND SIZES,
AND BY DECORATING THEM WITH A VARIETY
OF MATERIALS.

TIME REQUIRED: 45 MINUTES PER
ORNAMENT

MATERIALS NEEDED

Newspaper

Aluminum foil

Rubber gloves

Epoxy

Cotton swabs

Glass ornaments

6 mm colored beads

Copper wire

Pliers

Hot glue gun and glue sticks

Gold bullion

30 silver balls, ¼-inch diameter

Gold silk leaves

DIRECTIONS

STEP 1   Protect work surface with newspaper and foil;
put on rubber gloves.

STEP 2   Following manufacturer's instructions, squeeze
dime-size amount of epoxy onto foil. Mix epoxy with cotton swab and apply to bottom end of one ornament.
Quickly place bottom end of second ornament against
epoxy; adjust alignment, then hold together until they
adhere. Once stable, set aside to dry further.

OPTIONS: To decorate with colored beads, string them on
copper wire, curling ends with pliers to secure. Use glue
gun to adhere design.

   To decorate with gold bullion, remove both end caps
from the ornament. Wrap gold bullion around lip of one
opening. Gently stretch bullion down to other end cap and
wrap around that lip to attach. Continue to wrap bullion in
vertical strands around both bulbs, locking each vertical
strand at an end, until you create a thread-like cage;
replace end caps and add beads to finish each end.

   To decorate with silver balls and gold silk leaves, use
glue gun to adhere design.

Antiqued Treetop Star

STYLIZE SIMPLE OBJECTS BY APPLYING A GLOWING SURFACE OF GOLD LEAF
AND STIPPLED PAINT. THIS ANTIQUING METHOD WORKS ON ALMOST ANY
KIND OF MATERIAL: WOOD, GLASS, METAL, OR PAPER.

TIME REQUIRED: 1 HOUR

MATERIALS NEEDED

Aluminum foil

Paint brush

Gilding size

Treetop star form (a cardboard form is pictured, *left*)

Gold leaf

Acrylic paint: black and burnt sienna

Disposable plate or tray

Sea sponge

Paper towels

DIRECTIONS

STEP 1   Protect work surface with aluminum foil.

STEP 2   Following manufacturer's instructions for gilding size, brush a thin layer of size
onto one side of star and allow to dry until tacky.

STEP 3   Tear off a piece of gold leaf sheeting and place on surface of star. Smooth with
your hands to adhere. Add additional leaf until entire side is covered.

STEP 4   Repeat Steps 2 and 3 for back side of star. Set aside.

STEP 5   Mix 3 parts burnt sienna with 1 part black acrylic paint on disposable plate.

STEP 6   Dip corner of sea sponge in paint and blot on paper towel. Lightly tap sponge
over gilded star to create stippled effect; let dry. Turn star over and repeat on back side.
Let dry.

Poured Paint Ornaments

MAKE CLEAR GLASS ORNAMENTS GLOW WITH COLOR BY COATING THEIR INSIDES WITH BEAUTIFUL SHADES OF PAINT. USE BASIC PAINT COLORS, PALE METALLIC, OR PEARLESCENT COLOR TO CREATE LUSTROUS HOLIDAY SHADES.

TIME REQUIRED: 15 MINUTES
PER ORNAMENT

MATERIALS NEEDED
Newspaper
Clear glass ornaments
Acrylic paint
(use regular, metallic, or pearlized paint)
Paintbrush

DIRECTIONS

STEP 1   Protect work surface with newspaper.

STEP 2   Remove metal end cap from glass ornament to reveal opening.

STEP 3   Pour in one tablespoon of paint. Note: If paint is too thick to pour, dip paintbrush in paint, then wipe brush against opening of ornament to drain paint.

STEP 4   Place your finger over opening of ornament; shake until paint covers inside of ornament. If paint won't spread, add water, two drops at a time, until paint thins sufficiently.

STEP 5   Place ornament on newspaper to dry, rotating ornament for the first 5 minutes to ensure even coating. Allow to dry overnight.

STEP 6   Reinsert metal end cap.

Metallic Tape Ornaments

ADD PIZAZZ TO PLAIN GLASS ORNAMENTS BY APPLYING METALLIC GOLD GRAPHIC ART TAPE IN GEOMETRIC PATTERNS. FOR VARIETY, EXPERIMENT WITH METALLIC TAPES IN OTHER COLORS AND WIDTHS TO CREATE NEW DESIGNS.

TIME REQUIRED: 15 MINUTES PER ORNAMENT

MATERIALS NEEDED
Round glass ornaments
1 roll ¼-inch-wide gold metallic tape
Scissors

DIRECTIONS

STEP 1   Remove metal end cap from ornament.

STEP 2   Starting at top opening, run strip of tape down one side, across bottom point, and back up other side to top. Cut tape.

STEP 3   Repeat Step 2 to add desired amount of vertical stripes.

STEP 4   Run tape around middle of ornament to make horizontal stripe. Add more horizontal stripes as desired.

Gold Spiral Icicles

TWIRL GOLD PIPE CLEANERS TO MAKE FABULOUS ICICLES. THIS SIMPLE PROJECT IS EASY ENOUGH FOR CHILDREN TO MAKE.

TIME REQUIRED: 5 MINUTES PER ICICLE

MATERIALS NEEDED
Gold metallic pipe cleaners
1 dowel (or other round rod)

DIRECTIONS

STEP 1   Wrap a pipe cleaner around a dowel creating a long spiral.

STEP 2   Slide pipe cleaner off of dowel, leaving it coiled up. Gently pull ends apart to lengthen if needed.

STEP 3   Make loop at one end and hang on tree branch.

Miniature Beaded Fruit

INSPIRED BY THE BEADED FRUIT OF THE FIFTIES, THESE DAZZLING, RETRO-STYLE ORNAMENTS ARE SIMPLY MADE BY PINNING TRANSPARENT BEADS TO STYROFOAM SHAPES. MAKE SEVERAL AND PUT THEM INTO A FRUIT BOWL FOR A BEAUTIFUL CENTERPIECE.

TIME REQUIRED: 2 HOURS FOR EACH PIECE OF FRUIT

MATERIALS NEEDED

1 ½-inch Styrofoam plastic coated fruit:

1 apple	1 lemon
1 lime	1 orange
1 pear	1 banana
1 pomegranate	2 cherries

Aleene's Tacky Thin-bodied Glue
Watercolor paint brush
4 mm colored beads
(approximately 400 beads per piece of fruit)
1-cm long straight pins (one pin per bead; beads should slip easily onto pins but not slide off over head)
8 small silk leaves

DIRECTIONS

STEP 1   To prepare surface of fruit, apply thin layer of glue to small Styrofoam area using brush.

STEP 2   To decorate glued section, position one bead, hole side up, on fruit. Push straight pin through hole and into Styrofoam to secure bead. Repeat for each bead until glued section is covered. Position beads close together but not so tightly as to create buckling.

STEP 3   Continue gluing and pinning beads to fruit until Styrofoam is concealed. When fruit has dried, glue on silk leaf where natural stem would sprout.

Glitterball Ornaments

THESE FABULOUS ORNAMENTS SPARKLE AND SHINE AND COULD NOT BE EASIER TO MAKE. THIS IS A PERFECT PROJECT FOR CHILDREN. GLITTER IS AVAILABLE IN A RAINBOW OF COLORS.

TIME REQUIRED: ½ HOUR

MATERIALS NEEDED
Newspaper

Aluminum foil

Styrofoam balls

(pictured here: 2-3-inch balls)

Aleene's Tacky Thin-bodied Glue

Sponge brush

Glitter: gold, silver, red, lime green

(33 grams per two 3-inch balls)

Paper cups

Metal ornament end caps

DIRECTIONS

STEP 1   Protect work surface with newspaper. Lay out sheet of aluminum foil for drying.

STEP 2   Coat Styrofoam ball with glue using sponge brush or your fingers.

STEP 3   Sprinkle silver glitter over entire surface of ball. Allow to dry on aluminum foil for 15 minutes. Reuse extra glitter by picking up edges of newspaper to collect glitter in center. Pour extra glitter into paper cups.

STEP 4   Push wires of one ornament end cap into Styrofoam until secure. Add ornament hook.

STEP 5   To add stripes, hold ornament by end cap, and, using tip of glue bottle, apply 2 even circular stripes of glue, 1 inch from top and 1 inch from bottom. Sprinkle red glitter over glue to coat. Lightly shake off excess. Apply 2 more stripes of glue next to red ones; sprinkle gold glitter to coat.

STEP 6   Continue to decorate using stripes, curvy lines, swirls, and dots. Be sure to apply a new layer of glue for each additional color of glitter.

STEP 7   Hang ornament by hook to dry.

Wire Mesh Mini Lights

GIVE ORDINARY WHITE HOLIDAY LIGHTS THE WARM GLOW OF BRASS AND COPPER BY FOLDING FINE WIRE MESH INTO A SHADE FOR EACH BULB. THE LIGHTS CAN BE STRUNG AROUND YOUR CHRISTMAS TREE OR USED AS AN ACCENT FOR WINDOWS AND ENTRYWAYS.

TIME REQUIRED: 1 HOUR

MATERIALS NEEDED

2 x 1-foot copper wire mesh, 40 x 40 denier

Ruler

Scissors

2 x 1-foot brass wire mesh, 40 x 40 denier

(number of threads per square inch)

1 strand tree lights

DIRECTIONS

STEP 1   Cut strip of copper wire mesh 6 x 1 ¼-inches high.

STEP 2   Lay mesh horizontally on flat work surface. Fold down ¼ inch of top edge to form neat edge resembling a hem.

STEP 3   Turn mesh 45° to make vertical rectangle. Beginning at top, fold down ¼-inch hem.

STEP 4   Turn mesh over so that hem remains at top of vertical rectangle, but is face down on work surface. Fold down another ¼ inch. Continue turning and folding the mesh to create accordion-style folds.

STEP 5   With hem created in Step 2 folded toward outside, pull short ends gently to open accordion up and bend until ends meet to form a cylinder.

STEP 6   To attach short ends together, tuck last fold of one side into last fold of other side.

STEP 7   Holding ends together, slip bottom of mesh shade onto one light and pinch fold where seam comes together at base of light. Pinch additional folds around base to secure mesh in place around light.

STEP 8   Repeat Steps 1 to 7, alternating between copper and brass wire mesh, to decorate your entire strand of lights.

holiday desserts

6

*D*uring the holidays, desserts are the way to make the end of a wonderful meal as dazzling as the season. Here is a collection of delicious recipes that are as pleasing to be the eye as they are to the palate.

The anchor of this chapter is what else, but chocolate. Two old standbys, Chocolate Chip Cookies and Mocha Fudge Brownies, appear in their most delicious incarnation. A little more chocolate can be found in the sweet centers of the delightful Meringue Mushrooms. Also included are foolproof, easy directions to make Chocolate Holly Leaves and Chocolate-covered Strawberries.

For some traditional cooking, bake and build cozy gingerbread cottages with your children, or use the same spicy dough to cut out and decorate forties-style Old-fashioned Christmas Light Cookies. These brightly-colored cookies look charming when presented on a platter draped with silk cord.

Consider wrapping up some of the delicious sweets in "Holiday Desserts" as gifts. Aside from the fun of cooking up all of these wonderful delights, friends and family will truly appreciate the amount of time spent in the kitchen on their behalf. There is nothing better than a home filled with the aromas of holiday cooking.

Meringue Mushrooms

THESE DELECTABLE TREATS ARE SWEET AND COLORFUL, AND PERFECT INDIVIDUALLY AS A CONVERSATION PIECE AT EACH PLACE SETTING OR BOXED TOGETHER AS A GIFT.

TIME REQUIRED: 2 ½ HOURS

YIELD
30 mushrooms

INGREDIENTS AND MATERIALS NEEDED FOR MUSHROOMS
⅓ cup egg whites (about 3 large eggs)

1 teaspoon cream of tartar

½ teaspoon vanilla extract

2 ½ cups powdered sugar

Pastry bag with ½-inch round tip

2 baking sheets	Aluminum foil
Large bowl	Electric mixer

INGREDIENTS AND MATERIALS NEEDED FOR DECORATIONS
4 ounces semi-sweet chocolate

¼ teaspoon of vegetable shortening

⅛-inch writing tip (for pastry bag)

½-inch and ¼-inch paint brush

Red food coloring	Double boiler

DIRECTIONS

STEP 1 Preheat oven to 200° F.

STEP 2 Line two baking sheets with foil and set aside.

STEP 3 Beat egg whites and cream of tartar on medium speed for 2-3 minutes, until foamy. Increase speed to high and add vanilla. Beat until mixture forms stiff peaks, about 5 minutes.

STEP 4 Beat in powdered sugar on high speed in ¼ cup increments. Continue beating until mixture is thick and glossy. Place ¼ cup of mixture in plastic bag and place in refrigerator.

STEP 5 Fill pastry bag, using ½-inch round tip, with remaining meringue mixture.

STEP 6 To make mushroom stems, hold pastry bag perpendicular to baking sheet and squeeze until meringue is ¾-inch across. Continue squeezing and lift bag away from baking sheet; squeeze until stem is 1 ½-inches high and wider at bottom than top. Place stems 1-inch apart, and be sure to make a few extras (some tip over when baking and are unusable).

STEP 7 On new baking sheet, to make caps, squeeze until mixture is 1-inch to 1 ½-inches across and ¾-inch high. Make 30 round puffs. Use knife dipped in water to smooth away peak where pastry bag was pulled away.

STEP 8 Place both sheets in oven and bake for 45 minutes. Turn off oven earlier if you notice meringue turning golden. Leave baking sheets inside with doors closed for 15 more minutes.

TO DECORATE MERINGUE

STEP 1 Remove reserved meringue from refrigerator and set aside.

STEP 2 Using ¼-inch brush, paint entire top side of caps with red food coloring.

STEP 3 Place ⅛-inch tip on pastry bag, fill with reserved meringue, and squeeze out meringue dots over red painted caps.

STEP 4 Bake decorated caps in oven on 200° F for ½ hour.

STEP 5 With sharp knife, level tops of stems.

STEP 6 Melt chocolate and shortening in double boiler, stirring gently.

STEP 7 Using paint brush, coat underside of cap with ¼-inch layer of chocolate. Hold stem, centered, against chocolate underside of cap until it sets. Repeat to attach remaining stems and caps.

Gingerbread Cottage

THIS CHARMING COTTAGE-STYLE HOUSE IS GUARANTEED TO BE A SUCCESS—FOR NOVICE BUILDERS, ADULTS, AND CHILDREN ALIKE. THE RECIPE IS DESIGNED TO RESULT IN A SLIGHTLY RAISED DOUGH WITH ROUNDED EDGES, ENHANCING THE COZY, COTTAGE LOOK. THE FULL, PIPED DETAILS ADD FURTHER CHARM AND ARCHITECTURAL INTEREST, AND CAN CLEVERLY CONCEAL LESS-THAN-PERFECT BAKING RESULTS.

TIME REQUIRED: 3 HOURS

YIELD
3 cottages, 5 ¼-inches high and 3 ¾-inches wide

MATERIALS NEEDED FOR GINGERBREAD
3 cups all-purpose flour

1 teaspoon baking soda

2 teaspoons ground cinnamon

2 teaspoons ground ginger

1 teaspoon nutmeg

1 teaspoon cloves

1/2 cup butter

1/2 cup dark brown sugar, firmly packed

1 egg

1/2 cup unsulfured molasses

1 tablespoon lemon juice

Template (see page 99)

Lightweight cardboard (for pattern pieces)

Sturdy cardboard (for base of cottage)

2 large bowls

Flour sifter

Electric mixer

Measuring spoons

Rolling pin

Plastic wrap

Aluminum foil

Waxed paper

Knife

2 cookie sheets

Spatula

Wire racks

Pencil, ruler, and scissors

FOR ROYAL ICING
3 cups confectioner's sugar

1 egg white

½ teaspoon cream of tartar

½ teaspoon lemon extract

Pastry bag with ⅛-inch writing tip

Paint brush

Food coloring optional

DIRECTIONS FOR GINGERBREAD COTTAGE

STEP 1 Photocopy template on page 99. Trace outline onto lightweight cardboard and cut out pattern; set aside.

STEP 2 Sift flour, baking soda, and spices in mixing bowl; set aside.

STEP 3   In second bowl, beat butter and brown sugar until light and fluffy. Stir in egg, molasses, and lemon juice.

STEP 4   Slowly add half of dry ingredients; mix thoroughly. Add remaining dry ingredients and mix until fully blended.

STEP 5   Lay sheet of plastic wrap on counter. Scoop out half of dough with hands and form soft ball. Place ball on plastic wrap and flatten into disk; wrap with plastic and set aside. Repeat for remaining dough. Refrigerate dough 3 hours.

STEP 6   Preheat oven to 350° F. To make cottage sections, place dough disk on greased and floured cookie sheet. Position sheet of waxed paper on top of dough. Roll out dough to ³⁄₁₆-inch with rolling pin. Lift off waxed paper from rolled dough and discard.

STEP 7   Position cottage section templates on dough, positioning them to maximize use of dough. Use knife to trace around each template, being careful to make clean cuts. Continue repositioning and tracing templates on dough until you have enough for 2 sides, 2 roof pieces, and 1 front and 1 back piece. (This recipe will make up to 3 cottages.)

STEP 8   To make chimney, roll small handful of dough into 1 inch log. Turn round log into a square-shaped log by pressing against pan to form flat sides. Cut top of log straight across to make top of chimney; cut diagonally across bottom of log to match roof angle. If desired, cut out other architectural details from dough, such as shutters or windowsills, to add further style to your cottage.

STEP 9   Carefully pull extra dough away from cut out sections; store in refrigerator for reuse.

STEP 10   Bake gingerbread for 8-10 minutes; check frequently to avoid burning. When finished, remove gingerbread from oven and allow to cool on racks.

STEP 11   To make Royal Icing, use mixer to beat sugar, cream of tartar, lemon extract, and egg white until thick. Icing is ready if it holds a peak when knife is run through center of mixture. If icing is too soft, add more sugar; if too stiff, add teaspoon of water. Icing may be colored with drop of food coloring, as desired.

STEP 12   To assemble 1 cottage, line up baked sections on a flat work surface as follows: side, front, side, back, roof and roof.

STEP 13   Fill pastry bag with royal icing; set aside extra and cover with damp cloth to prevent hardening.

STEP 14   Stand up first side and front section, edges touching, and use icing to cement vertical joint between them. Repeat to join second side to front, using icing to cement joints. Complete cottage base by cementing remaining back section to 3-part base in same fashion.

STEP 15   Run icing along top edges of both sides and front and back peak sections. Position 1 roof section on icing, holding in place while second section is laid in place. Secure joint with icing; let cottage set for 1 hour.

STEP 16   Use icing to add welcome mat, door, windows, chimney, and any other custom-made pieces to cottage.

STEP 17   Refer to photograph as guide for decorating. Add squiggles to joint, icicles to roof line, bricks to chimney, and snow patch to roof. Smooth top of snow with wet paint brush.

TEMPLATES

peaked side (cut 2; front and back)

sides (cut 2)

roof (cut 2)

front window (cut 1)

side window (cut 1)

door (cut 1)

welcome mat (cut 1)

GINGERBREAD COTTAGE

TEMPLATE

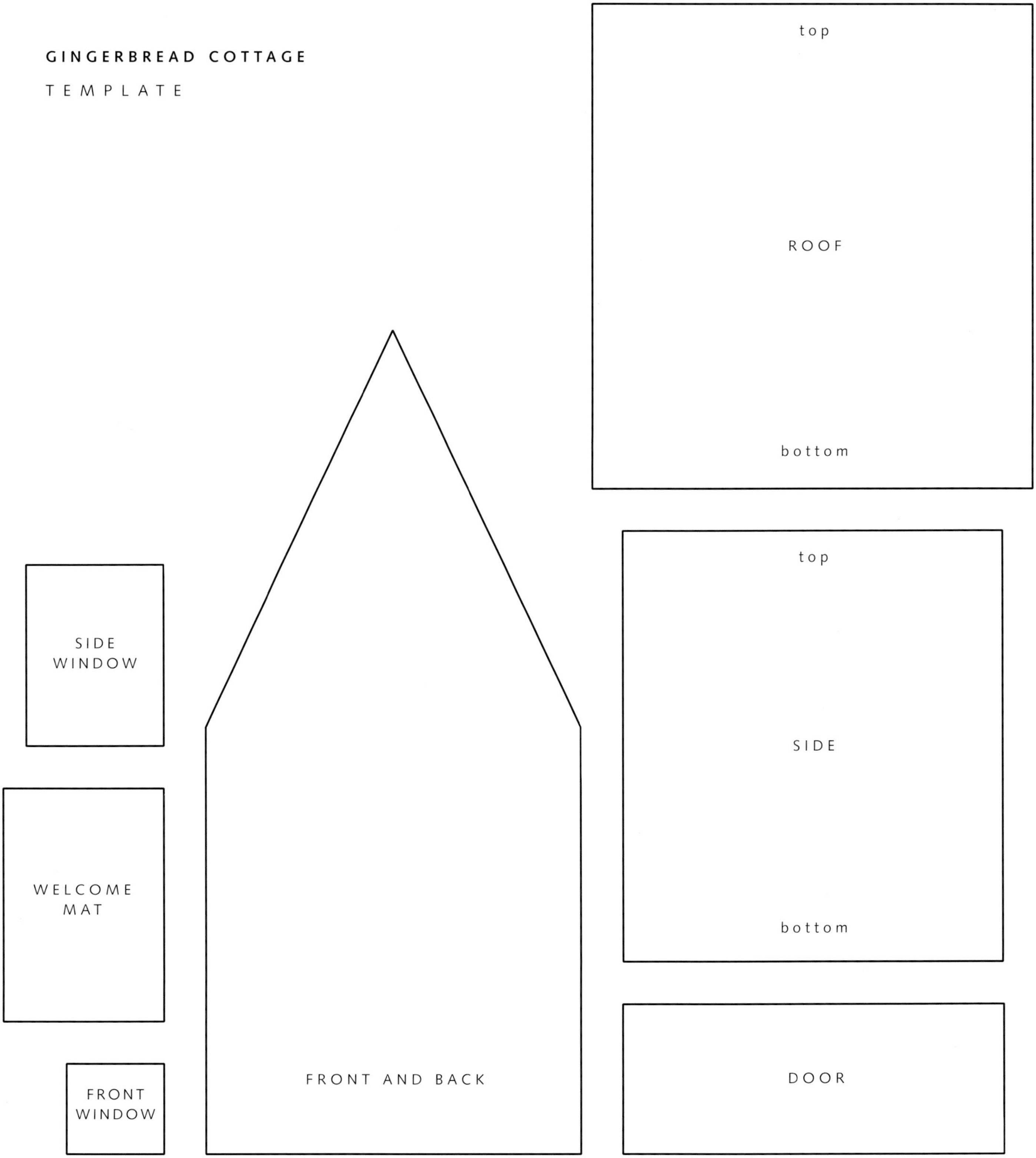

top

ROOF

bottom

top

SIDE

bottom

SIDE
WINDOW

WELCOME
MAT

FRONT
WINDOW

FRONT AND BACK

DOOR

99

Jellied Fruit Candies

THESE DELICIOUS, BITE-SIZED FRUIT CANDIES MAKE THE PERFECT AFTER DINNER SWEET. THE USE OF REAL FRUIT TO MAKE THESE CANDIES RESULTS IN A WONDERFUL BURST OF FLAVOR AND VIBRANT COLOR.

TIME REQUIRED: 1 HOUR PREPERATION TIME FOR EACH FLAVOR; 4 HOURS CHILLING TIME

YIELD

5 dozen of each color candy

INGREDIENTS AND MATERIALS NEEDED

FOR GREEN CANDIES

10 kiwis for 2 cups fruit puree
2 tablespoons fresh lemon juice
2 ¼ cups granulated sugar
4 envelopes Knox Unflavored Gelatine

FOR YELLOW CANDIES

4 oranges and 2 peaches
2 tablespoons fresh lemon juice
2 ¼ cups granulated sugar
4 envelopes Knox Unflavored Gelatine

FOR RED CANDIES

2 packages frozen raspberries
2 tablespoons fresh lemon juice
2 1/4 cups granulated sugar
4 envelopes Knox Unflavored Gelatine

3 11 x 7 x 1 ½-inch baking pans
1-inch cookie cutters (star, triangle, and flower)

Food processor
2-quart saucepan
Knife
Cutting board
Large bowl
Aluminum foil
Parchment paper

DIRECTIONS

STEP 1   Line 1 baking pan with parchment paper.

STEP 2   Peel kiwis. Blend in food processor with lemon juice until pureed. Place ½ cup fruit puree in bowl and set aside.

STEP 3   Place remainder of fruit puree in saucepan over medium heat. Stir in 2 cups sugar and bring to full boil. Remove from heat and set aside.

STEP 4   To fruit puree from Step 2, that has been set aside, stir in 4 pouches of gelatin. Let stand one minute.

STEP 5   Add hot puree to bowl of puree with gelatin and stir thoroughly. Pour in baking pan and refrigerate 4 hours.

STEP 6   Remove parchment paper and mixture from pan when firm. Use cookie cutters to cut shapes from candy. Roll triangles in remaining granulated sugar and arrange on serving plate.

STEP 7   Repeat Steps 1 through 6 to make yellow and red candies. Note: Oranges and peaches must be peeled, and peaches pitted.

Chocolate Holly Leaves

GIVE YOUR HOLIDAY DESSERTS A FESTIVE AND PROFESSIONAL TOUCH BY CROWNING THEM WITH REALISTIC-LOOKING CHOCOLATE LEAVES. THOUGH SHOWN HERE ON A CAKE, YOU CAN ALSO USE THESE LEAVES AS A GARNISH FOR FRESH FRUIT, ICE CREAM, AND OTHER PASTRIES.

TIME REQUIRED: 1/2 HOUR

YIELD
10 leaves

INGREDIENTS AND MATERIALS NEEDED
2 ounces semi-sweet chocolate

⅛ teaspoon vegetable shortening

4 plastic holly leaves

(Silk holly leaves, or other real, non-poisonous leaves such as rose, lemon, or ficus may also be used. Do not use real holly leaves.)

Double boiler

Paint brush

Aluminum foil

Baking sheet

DIRECTIONS

STEP 1   Cover baking sheet with foil and set aside.

STEP 2   Wash plastic holly leaves with soap and water. Let dry.

STEP 3   Heat chocolate and vegetable shortening in top of double boiler and stir until melted. Remove from heat.

STEP 4   Using a paint brush, spread a solid, even layer of chocolate over one side of leaf. Leave some of stem exposed for easy handling. Lay leaf on baking sheet. Repeat for remaining leaves.

STEP 5   Place baking sheet in refrigerator or freezer to chill. Remove when chocolate has set.

STEP 6   Hold a leaf at edges with fingertips of one hand. Using other hand, gently peel away plastic holly leaf starting at stem.

STEP 7   Arrange chocolate leaves and add silk berries or cranberries to garnish.

Chocolate-covered Strawberries

THIS SIMPLE TECHNIQUE FOR MAKING ONE OF THE WORLD'S MOST LUXURIOUS AND INDULGENT DESSERTS IS COMPLETELY FOOLPROOF. THESE GOURMET FRUITS ALSO MAKE A LOVELY HOSTESS GIFT.

TIME REQUIRED: 1 HOUR

YIELD

20 strawberries

INGREDIENTS AND MATERIALS NEEDED

8 ounces dark or semi-sweet chocolate

1 teaspoon vegetable shortening

20 ripe, firm strawberries

4 ounces white chocolate

Double boiler

Parchment paper

Baking sheet

Pastry bag with thin writing tip

Aluminum foil

DIRECTIONS

STEP 1   Wash strawberries and set on paper towel to dry.

STEP 2   Cover baking sheet with parchment paper and set aside.

STEP 3   Heat dark chocolate and ¾ teaspoon vegetable shortening in top of double boiler; stir until melted. Remove from heat.

STEP 4   Dip each strawberry in chocolate mixture and place on covered baking sheet. Set in refrigerator to chill.

STEP 5   Melt white chocolate and ¼ teaspoon vegetable shortening in top of double boiler. Remove from heat.

STEP 6   Place white chocolate in pastry bag with writing tip. Squeeze chocolate down to tip of bag and twist top of bag.

STEP 7   Remove strawberries from refrigerator. Using pastry bag, drizzle white chocolate, from left to right, over strawberries.

STEP 8   Return strawberries to refrigerator to chill. Cover with aluminum foil until ready to serve. These must be made and served the same day.

105

Old-fashioned Christmas Light Cookies

ROLL OUT, CUT, AND COLOR THESE DELICIOUS GINGERBREAD COOKIES TO RESEMBLE FORTIES-STYLE, CHRISTMAS LIGHTS. CREATE A UNIQUE SERVING PLATTER BY USING SILK CORD TO IMITATE THE WIRING OF REAL LIGHTS. EXTRA COOKIES CAN BE HUNG ON A CHRISTMAS TREE BY USING ROYAL ICING TO GLUE A HOOK TO THE BACK AND MAKING A LOOP OUT OF SILK CORD.

TIME REQUIRED: 2 HOURS

YIELD
4-5 dozen 1 ¾-inch cookies

INGREDIENTS AND MATERIALS NEEDED
Vegetable shortening for greasing
½ cup flour
Gingerbread recipe, page 97
Royal Icing recipe, page 98 (Step 11)
Red, blue, yellow, and green food coloring
Cookie sheet
For cookie template, use photo, *left*
Waxed paper
Rolling pin
Small saucers
Fine paintbrush
Red silk cord (optional)

DIRECTIONS

STEP 1   Photocopy the photo, *left,* and trace outline of one of the cookies onto lightwieght cardboard.

STEP 2   Preheat oven to 350° F. Grease and flour cookie sheet.

STEP 3   Prepare gingerbread dough. Cut a cookie template from lightweight cardboard, using the cookie pattern.

STEP 4   Place waxed paper over dough and roll out to ¼ inch on flat surface. Remove waxed paper and place cookie template on dough; cut out around shape, using knife. Repeat until all dough is used. Use spatula to move cookies to baking sheet.

STEP 5   Bake cookies 6-8 minutes; check frequently to avoid burning. When finished, transfer cookies to cooling racks.

STEP 6   Prepare Royal Icing recipe.

STEP 7   To decorate one cookie, apply even coat of royal icing on top surface, using knife dipped in water to ensure smooth coverage. Allow icing to harden. Repeat to ice remaining cookies.

STEP 8   Squeeze several drops of each food color onto saucer, one color per saucer. On additional saucer, mix equal parts red, blue, and green together to make outline color. Referring to cookie pattern for color placement and outlines, brush one color lightly over light bulb section, then draw boldface lines for bulb outline and crew-style end cap. Repeat to color remaining cookies.

STEP 9   To serve, arrange cookies on long platter, weaving silk cord around them to imitate electric wire.

Chocolate Chip Cookies

THESE ARE THE MOST DELICIOUS, RICH, AND BUTTERY CHOCOLATE CHIP COOKIES YOU WILL EVER MAKE.

TIME REQUIRED: 2 ½ HOURS

YIELD
Approximately 40 3 ½-inch cookies

INGREDIENTS AND MATERIALS NEEDED
¾ cup light corn syrup

½ cup butter (1 stick)

1 cup all-purpose flour

3 tablespoons granulated sugar

¼ teaspoon baking soda

1 large egg

1 ½ teaspoons vanilla extract

1 16-ounce bag of chocolate chips

2-quart saucepan

Mixing bowl

2 baking sheets

Spoon

Spatula

Measuring cups

Measuring spoons

Cooling racks

Aluminum foil

DIRECTIONS

STEP 1 In saucepan, bring corn syrup to a boil over medium heat.

STEP 2 Let boil for 3 minutes, stirring continuously. Add butter and continue to boil mixture for 2 minutes longer. Remove saucepan from heat and set aside to cool.

STEP 3 Sift together flour, sugar, and baking soda; set aside.

STEP 4 When corn syrup mixture is warm to cool, add in egg and vanilla, stirring vigorously.

STEP 5 Mix in dry ingredients. Mixture will be the consistency of pancake batter. Cover mixture with foil and place in refrigerator for ½ hour. Preheat oven to 325° F and grease cookie sheets.

STEP 6 Remove mixture from refrigerator and stir in chocolate chips.

STEP 7 Place rounded teaspoons of dough onto baking sheet, spacing 4 inches apart. Use back of spoon to flatten dough into disks of even thickness.

STEP 8 Place full sheet in oven and bake for 9 to 11 minutes. These cookies will brown quickly, so watch them carefully.

STEP 9 Using spatula, remove cookies from baking sheet and place on cooling rack. Be sure to allow baking sheets to cool completely before using them again.

Mocha Fudge Brownies

YOU WILL LOVE THE SUBTLE MOCHA UNDERTONE OF THESE MOIST, RICH, FUDGE BROWNIES AS THEY MELT IN YOUR MOUTH. SERVE THEM WITH COFFEE OR A LARGE GLASS OF ICE COLD MILK.

TIME REQUIRED: 1½ HOURS

YIELD
About 16 2-inch bars

INGREDIENTS AND MATERIALS NEEDED
¾ cup all-purpose flour

1 cup confectioner's sugar

½ cup mocha-flavored hot cocoa powder

¾ teaspoon baking powder

⅛ teaspoon salt

4 ounces of semi-sweet chocolate

6 tablespoons butter

1 ½ tablespoons dark corn syrup

2 eggs

1 ½ teaspoons vanilla extract

8-inch square baking pan

2 quart saucepan

large bowl

wooden spoon

DIRECTIONS

STEP 1   Preheat oven to 350° F. Grease baking pan.

STEP 2   In sauce pan, melt semi-sweet chocolate and butter over low heat. When chocolate and butter are melted, add corn syrup and stir. Remove from heat and let cool.

STEP 3   Sift flour, confectioner's sugar, hot cocoa powder, baking powder, and salt into large bowl. Set aside.

STEP 4   When chocolate mixture has cooled, use wooden spoon to stir in eggs and vanilla. Add dry ingredients and blend well.

STEP 5   Spoon into pan and place in oven. Bake 20 minutes for moist brownies, or 25 minutes for more firm brownies.

STEP 6   When done, place pan on cooling rack for 20 minutes. Cut into 2-inch squares and serve.

METRIC CONVERSION TABLE

LIQUID WEIGHTS

U.S. MEASUREMENTS	METRIC EQUIVALENTS
¼ teaspoon	1.23 ml
½ teaspoon	2.5 ml
¾ teaspoon	3.7 ml
1 teaspoon	5 ml
1 tablespoon (3 teaspoons)	15 ml
2 tablespoons (1 ounce)	30 ml
¼ cup	60 ml
⅓ cup	80 ml
½ cup	120 ml
⅔ cup	160 ml
¾ cup	180 ml
1 cup (8 ounces)	240 ml
2 cups (1 pint)	480 ml
3 cups	720 ml
4 cups (1 quart)	1 liter
4 quarts (1 gallon)	3 ¾ liters

TEMPERATURES

FARENHEIT	CELSIUS (CENTIGRADE)
32° F (water freezes)	0° C
200° F	95° C
212° F (water boils)	100° C
250° F	120° C
275° F	135° C
300° F (slow oven)	150° C
325° F	160° C
350° F (moderate oven)	175° C
375° F	190° C
400° F (hot oven)	205° C
425° F	220° C
450° F (very hot oven)	230° C
475° F	245° C
500° F (extremely hot oven)	260° C

DRY WEIGHTS

U.S. MEASUREMENTS	METRIC EQUIVALENTS
¼ ounce	7 grams
⅓ ounce	10 grams
½ ounce	14 grams
1 ounce	28 grams
1 ½ ounces	42 grams
1 ¾ ounces	50 grams
2 ounces	57 grams
3 ½ ounces	100 grams
4 ounces (¼ pound)	114 grams
6 ounces	170 grams
8 ounces (½ pound)	227 grams
9 ounces	250 grams
16 ounces (1 pound)	464 grams

LENGTH

U.S. MEASUREMENTS	METRIC EQUIVALENTS
⅛ inch	3 mm
¼ inch	6 mm
⅜ inch	1 cm
½ inch	1.2 cm
¾ inch	2 cm
1 inch	2.5 cm
1 ¼ inches	3.1 cm
1 ½ inches	3.7 cm
2 inches	5 cm
3 inches	7.5 cm
4 inches	10 cm

APPROXIMATE EQUIVALENTS

1 kilo is slightly more than 2 pounds

1 liter is slightly more than 1 quart

1 centimeter is approximately ⅜ inch

S O U R C E S

GENERAL CRAFT SUPPLIES:

Craft King
P.O. Box 90637
Lakeland, FL 33804
800-769-9494

Dick Blick Art Materials
P.O. Box 1267
Galesburg, IL 61402-1267
800-447-8192

Pearl Paint Company, Inc.
308 Canal Street
New York, NY 10013-2572
800-221-6845 x2297

Saks Art & Crafts
P.O. Box 510710
New Berlin, WI 53151
800-558-6696

BAKING:

NY Cake and Baking Distributor
56 West 22nd Street
New York, NY 10010
212-675-2253

A Cook's Wares
211 37th Street
Beaver Falls, PA 15010-2103
800-915-9788

BEADS:

Beadworks, Inc.
149 Water Street
Norwalk, CT 06854
203 852-9108

Toho Shoji
990 Sixth Avenue
New York, NY 10018
212-868-7466

SILK FLOWERS, FRUIT, AND FOLIAGE:

May Silk
16202 Distribution Way
Cerritos, CA 90703
800-282-7455

DRIED FLOWERS:

J&T Imports Dried Flowers
143 South Cedros #4
Solana Beach, CA 92075
619-481-9781

FLORAL SUPPLIES (FLORAL TAPE, PINS, FLORIST WIRE, WREATH FORMS)

A World of Plenty
P.O. Box 1153
Hermantown, MN 55810-9724
218-729-6761

GLITTER:

Jones Tones
33865 United Avenue
Pueblo, CO 81001
800-397-9667

HARDWARE:

True Value Hardware
Call 800-642-7392 for a store nearest you.

LIGHTING:

Just Bulbs
936 Broadway
New York, NY 10010-6063

PAPER:

Kate's Paperie
561 Broadway
New York, NY 10012
212-941-9816

SEWING NOTIONS, FABRIC, RIBBON, AND TRIM:

B&J Fabric
263 West 40th Street
New York, NY 10018
212-354-8150

Patterson Silks
36 East 14th Street
New York, NY 10003
212-929-7861

M&J Trim
1008 Sixth Avenue
New York, NY 10018
212-391-6200

WIRE:

Nasco Arts & Crafts
901 Janesville Avenue
P.O. Box 901
Fort Atkinson, WI 53538-0901
800-558-9595

///

Metalliferous
34 West 46th Street
New York, NY 10036
888-944-0909

HOME DECORATING:

Pottery Barn
P.O. Box 7044
San Francisco, CA 94120-7044
800-922-5507

IKEA
IKEA Catalog Department
185 Discovery Street
Colmar, PA 18915
800-434-4532

Pier One
7 East Jericho Tpk.
Huntington Station, NY 11746
516-424-9605